W9-BMR-956

America's Game

Boston Red Sox

Bob Italia

ABDO & Daughters
PUBLISHING

Published by Abdo & Daughters, 4940 Viking Dr., Suite 622, Edina, MN 55435.

Cover photo: Allsport
Interior photos: Wide World Photo, pages 1, 6, 7, 8, 13, 14, 21, 23,
24, 26, 27.
Allsport, page 5.

Edited by Kal Gronvall

Library of Congress Cataloging–in–Publication Data

Italia, Bob, 1955-
  Boston Red Sox / Bob Italia
    p. cm. — (America's game)
  Includes index.
  Summary: Focuses on key players and events in the history of the team that has played in Boston since 1901.
  ISBN 1-56239-686-2
  1. Boston Red Sox (Baseball team)—History—Juvenile literature.
[1. Boston Red Sox (Baseball team)—History. 2. Baseball—History.]
I. Title. II. Series.
GV875.B62I83 1997
796.357' 64' 0974461—dc20   96-38295
                                                CIP
                                                AC

Contents

Boston Red Sox

Perhaps no other team in Major League Baseball is better known for its postseason failures than the Boston Red Sox. But history paints a different portrait of these hard-luck losers. At the beginning of the century, Boston was the most successful team in baseball. They won six pennants and came away with victories in each World Series.

In the middle of the century, the Brooklyn Dodgers suffered more late-season and postseason collapses than even the gloomiest Red Sox fans could imagine. Though Boston in recent times has not only lost important games that it appeared to have won, it also has won major showdowns that it appeared to have lost.

Even more, the Red Sox have had enough players to fill an All-Star team. Cy Young, Babe Ruth, Tris Speaker, Lefty Grove, Joe Cronin, Jimmy Foxx, Ted Williams, Carl Yastrzemski, Jim Rice, Fred Lynn, Carlton Fisk, Roger Clemens, Wade Boggs, and Mo Vaughn have worn a Red Sox uniform.

Only one undeniable fact stands out through all Red Sox history: The franchise has not won a world championship since 1918. But then again, it is the team that traded Speaker and Ruth, turned down Jackie Robinson and Willie Mays, and allowed Fisk to leave the team while at the top of his game.

Boston has the core talent it needs to build a championship team. Should that core remain, Red Sox fans may soon witness that long-awaited World Championship.

Red Sox' pitcher Roger Clemens hurls a ball plateward in a game against the Oakland A's.

Red Sox' pitcher Denton "Cy" Young.

The Red Sox Are Born

Boston joined the American League (AL) in 1901. Until 1907, the new team had many names, starting with the "Americans," then the "Puritans," "Pilgrims," and "Somersets." Finally, in 1907, the National League's Boston Beaneaters dropped red from their uniform socks. That's when the AL team took the name Red Sox.

In their first year, Boston finished in second place, only four games behind the White Sox. Cy Young led the league in victories (33) and earned run average (1.62). Buck Freeman hit .345 with 114 RBIs. The same two shined the next season, when Young led the AL with 32 wins, while Freeman had a league-high 121 runs batted in (RBIs).

In 1903, Boston won its first pennant, finishing $14^{1}/_{2}$ games over the Athletics. Young led the league for the third time in a row with 28 wins, while Bill Dinneen and Long Tom Hughes notched 20 wins. Although his average slipped below .300, Freeman was still Boston's best hitter as he swatted 13 homers and knocked 104 runs—tops in the AL.

In mid-September, when it was clear that Boston and Pittsburgh would win their league's championships, they agreed to meet in a best-of-nine postseason competition.

The First World Series

In the first World Series, Boston lost three of the first four games to Pittsburgh. But then the club rallied behind Bill Dinneen, and won five out of eight games to capture the world championship. Dinneen's three wins included two shutouts. Boston captured the flag again in 1904, but the National League refused to meet in another World Series, claiming that the American League was "unworthy" of a championship battle.

Over the next seven years, Boston needed every victory that it could get. They ended up in the lower half of the division four times and finished last in 1906.

In 1912, Jake Stahl became manager. He led the team to its single greatest year ever as they won the pennant with a 105-47 record. Outfielder Tris Speaker and pitcher Joe Wood were the stars. Speaker batted .383 with 98 RBIs and an AL-best 10 homers. Wood notched a 34-5 record with a 1.91 earned run average (ERA). At one point in the season, he had 16 consecutive victories. Hugh Bedient and Buck O'Brien were also 20-game winners.

In the World Series against the New York Giants, Boston sought revenge for the 1904 snub. It was a tough battle, with Boston taking the title in seven games after jumping out to a 3-1 Series lead.

Left: Red Sox' outfielder Tris Speaker.

Landing
The Babe

A broken hand suffered by Wood sent Boston to fourth place the following season. Stahl was replaced by Bill Carrigan. Boston then acquired two of the minor league's top pitching talents: Babe Ruth and Ernie Shore.

Ruth recorded three-straight seasons of 18, 23, and 24 victories. In 1916, he led the AL in both ERA (1.75) and shutouts (9). Shore had his best year in 1915, when he won 19 with a 1.64 ERA. That same season, he and Ruth combined for 37 wins. Rube Foster posted another 19, and Wood led the league in ERA (1.49). Boston finished in first, $2^1/_2$ games ahead of Detroit. Speaker was the only hitter on the team who broke the .300 mark as he hit .322 . Duffy Lewis' 76 RBIs led the team.

In the World Series against the Phillies, Foster, Shore, and Leonard held Philadelphia to a team batting average of .182, as Boston took the championship in five games.

Babe Ruth takes a swing during spring training.

Another Championship

Boston's great pitching staff led them to another pennant in 1916. By then, Ruth had become the ace of the staff with 23 wins. Dutch Leonard and Carl Mays each posted 18 victories. But the hitting remained weak. Only third baseman Larry Gardner hit over .300. His 62 RBIs led the team.

In the World Series against Brooklyn, the Red Sox used their pitching to win in five games. Shore earned two wins and Gardner smacked two home runs while driving in six runs.

The Red Sox battled with the White Sox for first place in 1917. Then in September, Chicago pulled away and eventually took the pennant. Boston bounced back in 1918 to grab the AL flag on the strength of Mays' 21 wins and Ruth's 13 victories. Ruth also hit a league-leading 11 home runs with 66 RBIs, and recorded a team-high .300 batting average.

Facing the Chicago Cubs in the World Series, Ruth tossed a 1-0 shutout in the opening game, then went 7 1/3 more scoreless innings in Game 4. Ruth's scoreless-innings streak in the World Series swelled to 29 2/3—a record that stood until 1961. Mays also added a pair of 2-1 victories to give Boston its fifth world championship in as many tries.

The Curse Of The Bambino

In 1919, Ruth rewrote the game's offensive history. He led the league with 29 home runs and 114 RBIs. Despite his titanic efforts, the Red Sox finished in sixth place. Then, in a shocking move, Boston sold the outfielder-pitcher for financial reasons to the New York Yankees for $100,000.

Ruth's sudden departure marked the beginning of a long championship drought during which the team would not win a single World Series title. At the time, outraged Boston fans called the sale of Ruth "the crime of the century." As time went on, Red Sox fans watched in agony as the Babe helped build a Yankee dynasty while becoming a baseball legend. Ruth's sale would eventually be known as "The Curse of the Bambino" (*bambino* is the Italian word for "babe")—and would haunt the club throughout its history.

With Ruth gone, the Red Sox fell into the abyss. The team finished in fifth place in 1920 and 1921, then finished in the cellar eight out of the following nine years. The team also went 15 consecutive seasons without reaching the .500 mark. Only in 1934 did they manage to boost themselves into fourth place.

Turning The Team Around

 New owner Tom Yawkey worked hard to turn the team around. He hired Hall of Fame second baseman Eddie Collins as general manager, then acquired players such as pitcher Lefty Grove and shortstop Joe Cronin, who also acted as manager. The Hall of Famer would play and manage for Boston until 1948.

Following the 1935 season, the Sox added slugger Jimmie Foxx. In Foxx's first four years with Boston, he hit between 35 and 50 home runs and drove in between 105 and 175 runs. In 1938, the slugger won his third Most Valuable Player (MVP) Award while leading the American League in batting (.349), RBIs (175), and walks (119). He also smacked 50 homers, 33 doubles, and scored 139 runs.

Despite Foxx's sparkling years, the Red Sox could not win a pennant. The closest Boston came in the 1930s were two second-place finishes in 1938 and 1939.

Though the team was absent from postseason play, Red Sox fans were entertained by two of the most important players in franchise history. In 1938, second baseman Bobby Doerr took over a position he would hold until he retired after the 1951 season. One of the best offensive second basemen ever, Doerr had six seasons of more than 100 RBIs and 12-straight years of double figures in homers. In 1944, the Hall of Famer won the MVP Award after hitting a career-high .325.

Ted Williams

Despite Doerr's All-Star performance, he could not remain in the spotlight. That honor was passed in 1939 to rookie Ted Williams—considered by experts as one of baseball's greatest hitters.

Williams' statistics in his 19 years with the Red Sox were amazing. He became a lifetime .344 hitter with a .634 career-slugging average. He also won six batting titles—including one in 1941, when his .406 batting average marked the last time a major league player reached the .400 level. Williams led the AL in home runs four times, in RBIs four times, in runs scored six times, in doubles twice, in walks eight times, and in slugging average nine times.

Even more amazing, Williams posted all his incredible numbers despite missing almost six full seasons at the peak of his career to World War II, the Korean War, and injuries. But not even two wars could stop Williams. In 1958, he became the oldest player to win a batting crown (40 years and 28 days). In the final at-bat of his career (1960), he smacked his 29th home run of the season.

With Williams leading the offense, the Red Sox became contenders in the 1940s. After World War II ended (1945), Boston got its key players back. In 1946, they won 104 games for the second-best season in franchise history. Even more, they made a joke of the 1946 pennant race, winning the title by 12 games. Williams, of course, was the star. He recorded a .342 average with 38 homers and 123 RBIs. Doerr contributed 116 RBIs, and first baseman Rudy York knocked in 119 runs.

The World Series against the St. Louis Cardinals was supposed to be a walk in the park for the Red Sox. But unfortunately, it turned into a seven-game war. In the finale, St. Louis grabbed a 3-1 lead in the fifth inning. But Boston came back in the top of the eighth to tie the score. Enos Slaughter eventually scored the winning run for the Cardinals. For the tormented Boston fans, the curse of the Bambino had come alive.

Williams won the Triple Crown in 1947. But the team didn't return to the postseason because of injuries to its starting pitching staff. Following the season, Cronin became general manager. Long-time Yankees' manager Joe McCarthy was hired as the new skipper.

In 1949, Boston, Cleveland, New York, and Philadelphia battled for most of the season for first place. It finally ended with the Red Sox and Indians tied for the lead. In the winner-take-all playoff game, Cleveland won 8-3. The next year, Boston lost out to the Yankees for the pennant on the last game of the regular season. The curse, it seemed, was still with the team.

Outfielder Ted Williams at batting practice in 1941.

Carl Yastrzemski smacks a homer during a game against the New York Yankees.

The Middle Of The Pack

Boston didn't come close to winning the pennant in the 1950s. In fact, it was not until 1967 that Boston returned to postseason competition.

Williams broke his elbow during the 1950 All-Star Game, then got drafted into military service for the Korean War. By the end of the decade, he finally showed signs of aging. Boston usually stayed above .500, but never advanced past the middle of the standings.

The 1950s also had their bright spots. In 1950, Billy Goodman won the batting title—the only 20th-century utility player to do so. That same year, Boston became the most recent club to have a team batting average above .300.

The next decade, Boston experienced an eight-year stretch in which they lost more games than they won. When Williams retired in 1960, the Red Sox suffered from a power outage. One bright spot was Pete Runnels, who won the batting crown in 1960 and 1962. The best pitcher was Bill Monbouquette, who won 20 games in 1963, even though the Sox finished in seventh place.

Yaz & Company

In 1961, Carl Yastrzemski took over Williams' left field position. It marked the start of a 23-year Hall-of-Fame career played in Boston. Yastrzemski led the league in every major offensive category except triples and steals in one year or another. In 1967, he won the Triple Crown and the MVP Award with 44 homers, 121 RBIs, and a .326 batting average. That year he also led the league with 112 runs while smacking 31 doubles. By the time he retired, Yaz had won three batting titles and collected 3,419 career hits. His lifetime 646 doubles, 1,844 RBIs, and 1,845 bases on balls all ranked him within the top 10.

Much was expected from Tony Conigliaro after he joined the team in 1964 and smacked 24 home runs. The following season, the 20-year-old outfielder became the youngest player ever to lead the AL in homers when he belted 32.

After more success in 1966, Conigliaro was on his way to his best season ever in 1967. But then tragedy struck. He was beaned in August by Jack Hamilton of the Angels and suffered serious vision and balance problems. As a result, Conigliaro remained on the bench until 1969. Then he returned to bang out 20 homers. In 1970, Conigliaro appeared to be fully recovered when he hit 36 homers and drove in 116 runs. But his power display did not last, and he was traded to California.

The Pennant At Last!

At the end of the 1966 season, Dick Williams took over as manager. In 1967, Williams led the club through one of the tightest pennant races in the history of baseball. When it was over, Boston finished just one game ahead of Detroit and Minnesota and only three ahead of Chicago. More impressively, the Red Sox became the only team in the 20th century to win the pennant by picking up nine places in the standings from one year to the next.

Yastrzemski tore up the league with his Triple Crown season, and Jim Lonborg's 22 wins were tops in the AL. In Boston's first World Series in more than 20 years, the Red Sox faced an old nemesis: the Cardinals. Once again, the Red Sox lost in seven games as St. Louis fireballer Bob Gibson won three times. Much to the dismay of Red Sox fans, the Babe's curse had not loosened its grip on the club.

In 1968, Yastrzemski successfully defended his batting title. But his .301 average was a record-low for a hitting champion. His power numbers also fell. But Yaz's decline was nothing compared to that of his teammates. Two weeks before the end of a losing 1969 season, Williams was fired.

The 1970s

The 1970s were the club's best decade since the championship days of the Babe in the 1910s. But though they never finished below third place in the Eastern Division, Boston won only one AL title.

In 1972, the Red Sox were one-half game behind Detroit when a players' strike ended the season. Pitcher Luis Tiant and catcher Carlton Fisk emerged as the new Boston stars.

Tiant led the league in 1972 with his 1.91 ERA, then went on to win 20 games in 3 seasons and 18 in a fourth. Fisk, the best catcher in the history of the team, took over the regular job with a .293 average, 22 homers, and a league-leading 9 triples. Through the rest of the 1970s, Fisk would battle the Yankees' Thurman Munson for the title of best catcher in the AL.

In 1975, outfielders Fred Lynn and Jim Rice arrived in Boston. Lynn became the only major leaguer to win both Rookie of the Year and MVP Awards in the same year when he hit for a .331 average, smacked 21 homers, and drove in 105 runs. Rice was equally impressive with his .309 average, 22 home runs, and 102 RBIs. With the two mighty rookies leading the way, the Sox won the division. In the American League Championship Series (ALCS), Boston swept Oakland in three games. Tiant pitched a three-hitter in one contest while Yastrzemski played outstanding offense and defense. But the Sox would have to go into the World Series without Rice, who had broken his arm in a late-season game against the Tigers. Silently, Red Sox fans wondered if the curse was at work again.

In 1901, Cy Young led the American League with 33 wins and a 1.62 ERA.

In 1912, outfielder Tris Speaker batted .383 with 98 RBIs and an AL-best 10 homers.

As a pitcher in 1916, Babe Ruth led the AL in both ERA (1.75) and shutouts (9).

Outfielder Ted Williams won the Triple Crown of baseball in 1947.

During his 23-year baseball career, Carl Yastrzemski won three batting titles and collected 3,419 hits.

In 1983, Wade Boggs won the first of his five batting championships in Boston with a .361 average.

In 1985, Cy Young and MVP Award winner Roger Clemens set a major league record by striking out 20 batters in one game.

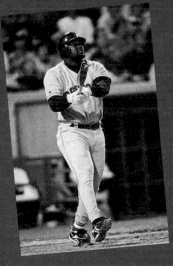

In 1995, MVP Mo Vaughn hit 39 home runs and knocked in 126 runs.

Fisk's Home Run

The World Series against the Cincinnati Reds became one of the most memorable in postseason history. By the time the sixth game at Fenway Park rolled around, the Sox were down three games to two in the Series. The Reds held a 6-3 lead into the eighth inning, when Bernie Carbo came off the bench to tie the game with a dramatic three-run pinch-homer.

For the next three innings, the teams could not push across another run. Then, shortly after midnight in the bottom of the 12th inning, Carlton Fisk launched a shot down the left field line that landed inches fair over the Green Monster. The homer became part of baseball lore as Fisk frantically jumped and waved for the ball to remain fair as it twisted along the foul line. It seemed as though the curse had finally been lifted. But Joe Morgan's eighth-inning single in the final game gave Cincinnati the world championship.

In November 1976, Boston signed reliever Bill Campbell in the hopes of improving the team. But Boston fell to third with an 83-79 record as Don Zimmer replaced Darrell Johnson as manager before the season ended. In September 1977, the Red Sox were sold to a syndicate.

Zimmer guided Boston to its most successful back-to-back years since the championship days of Ruth. In 1977, Campbell silenced his critics by winning 13 games and saving 31 more. But it was the offensive explosion that stole the headlines. Rice hit a league-best 39 homers, first baseman George Scott smacked 33, third baseman

Butch Hobson banged out 30, Yaz had 28, and Fisk contributed 26. Rice, Hobson, Yaz, and Fisk also had 100 or more RBIs each. The Sox finished with an impressive 97-64 record. But it was only good for a second-place tie.

Carlton Fisk jumps on home plate after hitting the homer that won Game 6 of the 1975 World Series for the Red Sox.

The Collapse

In 1978, Boston ran up a $14\frac{1}{2}$ -game lead over the Yankees by mid-July. Pitchers Dennis Eckersley (20 wins) and Mike Torrez (16 wins) led the way. Rice led the AL in home runs (46) and RBIs (139) and the most total bases (406) any player has accumulated since 1948.

Boston looked as though they had their strongest team ever. But then the team went into a tailspin in the second half of the season, at one point losing 14 of 17 games. That allowed the New York Yankees to sneak back into the pennant race. Even worse, the Red Sox suffered a four-game September sweep at the hands of the Yankees at Fenway Park. The curse had struck again!

The Yankees eventually seized a $3\frac{1}{2}$ -game lead over Boston, and it looked as though another promising season would end in disaster. But the Red Sox fought back to win eight in a row and earned a tie at the end of the regular season. With everything on the line in a one-game playoff, Torrez took a 2-0 lead into the seventh inning. Then—unbelievably—light-hitting New York shortstop Bucky Dent lifted a fly ball into the screen above the Green Monster for a three-run home run and a 3-2 New York lead. Red Sox fans could only shake their heads and mutter something about a trade made long ago. Now they would have to face the inevitable conclusion. Reliever Bob Stanley gave up two more runs, while the Yankees held off Red Sox rallies in the final two innings. A 99-64 record was not good enough to win the division.

Wade Boggs leaps to avoid colliding with a baserunner.

The 1980s

Zimmer guided the Sox to another successful season in 1979 when the team finished 91-69. Despite the impressive record, Boston slipped to third place. Zimmer survived to within a few games of the end of the 1980 season when the team finished with an 83-77 mark, but then was replaced by Ralph Houk. On September 12, 1979, Yaz cracked his 3,000th hit, becoming the first American Leaguer to reach that level while also collecting 400 home runs. Lynn and Rice continued to pound the baseball, as Lynn won the batting title with a .333 average, while Rice won the RBI duel 130-122. Both clouted 39 homers.

During the 1980-81 offseason, Burleson, Hobson, Lynn, and Fisk left the team. In the strike-shortened season of 1981, newcomer Carney Lansford peppered balls off the Green Monster to win the batting crown (.336).

In 1983, Wade Boggs won the first of his five batting championships in Boston with a .361 average, while Rice led the AL with 39 homers and 126 RBIs. The following year, center fielder Tony Armas led in homers (43) and RBIs (123). Despite such offensive displays, Boston remained stuck in the middle of the Eastern Division. Houk quit at the end of the 1984 season. John McNamara replaced him.

In 1985, Boggs won another batting championship with a .368 average. But Boston's 81-81 record left the team in fifth place. A few days before the 1986 season began, the Red Sox signed designated hitter Don Baylor. He led the team with 31 home runs and 94 RBIs as Boston surprised everyone by notching a 95-66 mark while capturing the AL pennant.

Baylor wasn't the only star. Fireballer Roger Clemens exploded against the league, winning his first 14 decisions. He finished with a 24-4 record and an AL-leading ERA of 2.48—making him an easy winner of both the Cy Young and MVP Awards. Just as important, Clemens often stopped losing skids whenever it was his turn to pitch. On April 19th, "The Rocket" established a major league record by striking out 20 batters in a game against Seattle.

But in the ALCS against the California Angels, not even the powerful Clemens seemed immune to the curse. He failed in two starts in the first four games. Boston entered the ninth inning of the fifth game three runs down—and only three outs away from elimination. Once again, Red Sox fans prepared for the inevitable.

But then something incredible happened. In one of the most dramatic comebacks in league history, Boston erased California's lead on two-run homers by Baylor and newcomer Dave Henderson. Although the Angels came back to tie the contest in the bottom of the inning, Henderson hit the game-winning sacrifice fly in the 11th inning. Inspired by the comeback, Boston hammered California pitching to win the next two games 10-4 and 8-1 in the last two games to win its first pennant since 1975.

Red Sox' designated hitter Don Baylor.

The Ultimate Boston Nightmare

The World Series against the Mets turned out to be even more dramatic than the ALCS. In the sixth game at New York, with the Sox leading the Series 3-2, the teams battled evenly through nine innings. Then Henderson ignited a two-run rally in the 10th with another home run. Boston fans thought the curse was finally over. But what followed became the ultimate Red Sox nightmare.

With only three outs to go for a world championship, Schiraldi retired the first two batters quickly. He was one strike away from getting pinch-hitter Gary Carter—when the curse struck again. Carter, pinch-hitter Kevin Mitchell, and Ray Knight singled. Stanley came in to yield the tying run on a wild pitch, and Mookie Wilson hit a grounder through first baseman Bill Buckner's legs to score the winning tally. It was one of the most agonizing losses in World Series history. Both Boston relievers returned in Game 7, but they lost another Boston lead while handing the Mets the world championship. Somewhere, the Babe was laughing.

In 1987, Boggs earned another batting title while Clemens chalked up another 20 wins. But Boston's fifth-place finish was disappointing. In 1988, Boggs won another batting title with a .366 average, and became the first player in baseball history to record six-straight seasons of at least 200 hits.

At the 1988 All-Star break, Boston fired McNamara and replaced him with minor league manager Joe Morgan. He led the Sox to 12-straight victories and 19 wins out of 20 games. Boston beat Detroit for the division title by one game with an 89-73 record. But the ALCS against Oakland was a disaster, as Bruce Hurst lost twice during a four-game sweep.

The 1980s finished on a low note, as Rice and Stanley were released. But Boston rebounded in 1990 to take yet another division title. Clemens (21 wins, 1.93 ERA) and Mike Boddicker (17 victories) had solid seasons. But the return matchup against the Athletics in the ALCS ended in another postseason disappointment. Boston lost four-straight contests, scoring only one run in each game.

After a second-place finish in 1991, the club fired Morgan and made former third baseman Butch Hobson his successor. The team collapsed completely, finishing last for the first time since 1932. The lone highlight of the season occurred on June 15, when reliever Jeff Reardon earned his 342nd career-save to break the record held by Rollie Fingers. Before the end of the year, Reardon was sent to Atlanta. In the offseason, Boggs signed with the Yankees.

The Sox improved little the next two years under Hobson. One bright spot was first baseman Mo Vaughn, who became one of the league's best power hitters. Hobson was fired following the 1994 season after becoming the first Boston manager in seven decades to earn three consecutive losing records. Kevin Kennedy replaced him.

Relief pitcher Jeff Reardon cheers as Boston wins the AL East Championship.

Mo Vaughn watches his two-run home run during a game against the Chicago White Sox.

One Mo' Title

In 1995, the Red Sox surprised everyone when they won the East Division race by seven games. MVP Vaughn hit 39 home runs and knocked in 126 runs. But it was the roster adjustments that made the difference as 50 players wore the Boston uniform at one time or another. The most important additions were slugger Jose Canseco (24 home runs), and pitchers Eric Hanson (15 wins) and Tim Wakefield (16 wins). Boston also added relief ace Rick Aguilera, who recorded 20 saves.

The division series, however, was another familiar story to Boston fans. Vaughn and Canseco went hitless in a combined 27 at-bats as the Red Sox lost to Cleveland in three games. The sweep left Boston with 13-straight losses in postseason play.

Ending The Curse

With Mo Vaughn and Roger Clemens representing the heart and soul of the Red Sox, Boston has the talent and the experience it needs to build a championship team. If management ignores past trends, keeps its team intact, and obtains some pitching help, Red Sox fans may soon see an end to the postseason curse that has plagued Boston since 1919.

Glossary

All-Star: A player who is voted by fans as the best player at one position in a given year.

American League (AL): An association of baseball teams formed in 1900 which make up one-half of the major leagues.

American League Championship Series (ALCS): A best-of-seven-game playoff with the winner going to the World Series to face the National League Champions.

Batting Average: A baseball statistic calculated by dividing a batter's hits by the number of times at bat.

Earned Run Average (ERA): A baseball statistic which calculates the average number of runs a pitcher gives up per nine innings of work.

Fielding Average: A baseball statistic which calculates a fielder's success rate based on the number of chances the player has to record an out.

Hall of Fame: A memorial for the greatest baseball players of all time, located in Cooperstown, New York.

Home Run (HR): A play in baseball where a batter hits the ball over the outfield fence scoring everyone on base as well as the batter.

Major Leagues: The highest ranking associations of professional baseball teams in the world, currently consisting of the American and National Baseball Leagues.

Minor Leagues: A system of professional baseball leagues at levels below Major League Baseball.

National League (NL): An association of baseball teams formed in 1876 which make up one-half of the major leagues.

National League Championship Series (NLCS): A best-of-seven-game playoff with the winner going to the World Series to face the American League Champions.

Pennant: A flag which symbolizes the championship of a professional baseball league.

Pitcher: The player on a baseball team who throws the ball for the batter to hit. The pitcher stands on a mound and pitches the ball toward the strike zone area above the plate.

Plate: The place on a baseball field where a player stands to bat. It is used to determine the width of the strike zone. Forming the point of the diamond-shaped field, it is the final goal a base runner must reach to score a run.

RBI: A baseball statistic standing for *runs batted in.* Players receive an RBI for each run that scores on their hits.

Rookie: A first-year player, especially in a professional sport.

Slugging Percentage: A statistic which points out a player's ability to hit for extra bases by taking the number of total bases hit and dividing it by the number of at bats.

Stolen Base: A play in baseball when a base runner advances to the next base while the pitcher is delivering the pitch.

Strikeout: A play in baseball when a batter is called out for failing to put the ball in play after the pitcher has delivered three strikes.

Triple Crown: A rare accomplishment when a single player finishes a season leading their league in batting average, home runs, and RBIs. A pitcher can win a Triple Crown by leading the league in wins, ERA, and strikeouts.

Walk: A play in baseball when a batter receives four pitches out of the strike zone and is allowed to go to first base.

World Series: The championship of Major League Baseball played since 1903 between the pennant winners from the American and National Leagues.

Index

M

Mays, Carl 9
Mays, Willie 4
McCarthy, Joe 13
McNamara, John 23, 26
Minnesota Twins 16
Mitchell, Kevin 25
Monbouquette, Bill 14
Morgan, Joe 20
Morgan, Manager Joe 26
Munson, Thurman 17

N

New York Giants 7
New York Mets 25
New York Yankees 10, 13, 17, 22, 26

O

Oakland Athletics 6, 17,26
O'Brien, Buck 7

P

Philadelphia Phillies 8, 13

R

Reardon, Jeff 26
Rice, Jim 4, 17, 20, 21, 22, 23, 26
Robinson, Jackie 4
Runnels, Pete 14
Ruth, Babe 4, 8, 9, 10, 20, 25

S

Schiraldi, Calvin 25
Scott, George 20
Shore, Ernie 8, 9
Slaughter, Enos 13
Speaker, Tris 4, 7, 8
St. Louis Cardinals 12, 13, 16
Stahl, Jake 7, 8
Stanley, Bob 22, 25, 26

T

Tiant, Luis 17
Torrez, Mike 22

V

Vaughn, Mo 4, 26, 27, 28

W

Wakefield, Tim 27
Williams, Dick 16
Williams, Ted 4, 12, 13, 14, 15, 16
Wilson, Mookie 25
Wood, Joe 7, 8
World Series 4, 7, 8, 9, 10, 12, 16, 17, 20, 25
World War II 12

Y

Yastrzemski, Carl 4, 15, 16, 17
Yawkey, Tom 11
York, Rudy 12
Young, Cy 4, 6, 24

Z

Zimmer, Don 20, 23